From: _____

To: _____

Copyright © 2020 by Tomika Carter

Written by Tomika Carter
Illustrations by Tonya Rouse
Colored by Eman Faulkner

All rights reserved. No part of this book may be used or reproduced in any matter whatsoever without the prior written permission of the author.

Robert Thomas Publishing
Washington DC

For more information on products and Robert Thomas Publishing, visit us online at
www.robertthomaspublishing.com

Then God said, "Let us make man in our image, in our likeness.." So God created man in his own image, in the image of God he created him; male and female he created them." **(Genesis 1:26–27)**

This book is dedicated to every little boy and girl in the world. You were created by God and God doesn't make mistakes.
You are OK!

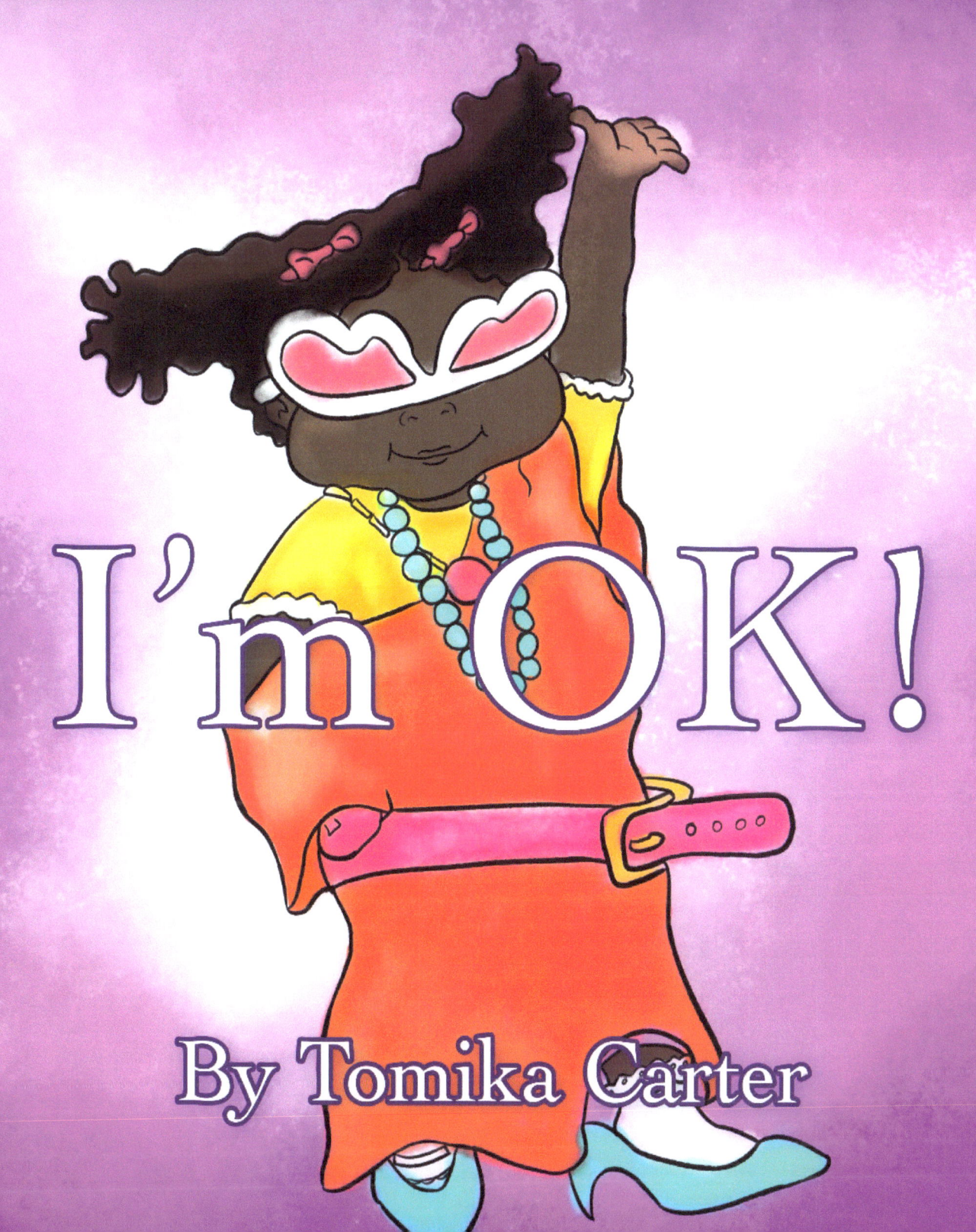

I Am Beautiful!

I Am Smart!

I Am Courageous!

And I Do My Part!

I Am Unique In Every Way!

Jesus Loves Me!

And I'm OK!

The End

I'm Ok Lyrics

I am beautiful
I am smart
I am courageous
And I do my part
I am unique
In every way
Jesus Loves me
And I'm Ok

I am special
Yes I'm great
I am fearfully and
Wonderfully made
There is nothing
That I can't do
Jesus God Loves me
And that's the truth

Even when I make mistakes
Or things don't go my way
I know that I can trust in God
Cause he knows what's best for me

I am beautiful
I am smart
I am courageous
And I do my part
I am unique
In every way
Jesus Loves me
And I'm ok

I am beautiful
I am smart
I am courageous
And I do my part
I am unique
In every way
Jesus Loves me
And I'm ok

I'm Ok

Lyrics by Tomika Carter
Sung by The Barbers Singers

About the author

Tomika Arnold-Carter is an author and owner of Robert Thomas Publishing. Tomika's books include the children's book "Who Gets The Glory" and finance book "Apples 2 Apples". For more information about Tomika, visit her website www.robertthomaspublishing.com, follow her on Instagram @robertthomaspublishing or like her Facebook fan page at www.facebook.com/robertthomaspublishing

A Word from the Author

Dear Reader,

Thank you for reading I'm Ok, I hope you were able to download, listen and enjoy the song as well. Please take a moment and leave a review on **www.amazon.com**. We would love to hear how this book and song inspired you and your family.